IT'S GREAT TO BE A FAN IN
OHIO

by Todd Kortemeier

CAVALIERS

SPALDING

CINCINNATI
19

FOCUS READERS

www.focusreaders.com

Focus Readers is distributed by North Star Editions:
sales@northstareditions.com | 888-417-0195

Produced for Focus Readers by Red Line Editorial.

Photographs ©: Tony Dejak/AP Images, cover (top), 1 (top); Nati Harnik/AP Images, cover (bottom left), 1 (bottom left); Ric Tapia/Icon Sportswire/AP Images, cover (bottom right), 1 (bottom right); Scott W. Grau/Icon Sportswire/AP Images, 4–5; NativeStock/North Wind Picture Archives, 7; Library of Congress, 9, 12–13; Red Line Editorial, 11, 35; Frank Jansky/Icon Sportswire/AP Images, 15; Harold P. Matosian/AP Images, 17; berni0004/Shutterstock Images, 19; Aaron Doster/Cal Sport Media/AP Images, 21; Tom DiPace/AP Images, 23; John Korduner/Icon Sportswire/AP Images, 24–25; aceshot1/Shutterstock Images, 27; Aspen Photo/Shutterstock Images, 29; Pro Football Hall of Fame/AP Images, 30–31; Debby Wong/Shutterstock Images, 33, 36–37; Tim Hutchison/Shutterstock Images, 39; John Minchillo/AP Images, 43; Jeff Haynes/AP Images, 45

ISBN
978-1-63517-935-4 (hardcover)
978-1-64185-037-7 (paperback)
978-1-64185-239-5 (ebook pdf)
978-1-64185-138-1 (hosted ebook)

Library of Congress Control Number: 2018932002

Printed in the United States of America
Mankato, MN
May, 2018

ABOUT THE AUTHOR

Todd Kortemeier is a sports journalist, children's book author, and massive sports fan from Minnesota. He has authored dozens of sports books for young people and has also covered US Olympic sports and the NHL. Todd and his wife live near Minneapolis with their dog.

TABLE OF CONTENTS

CHAPTER 1

GREAT RIVER

Ohio is one of the country's great places to watch sports. It's the state where professional football began. It's also home to three big cities with major league teams. In addition, several smaller towns and cities have proud high school, college, and minor league traditions. Ohio also boasts a major university with a highly successful athletics department. This sports culture reflects the state's culture, **economy**, and geography.

Ohio fans have a lot to cheer for, such as the successful Ohio State University football team.

The first people to live in the area now called Ohio were American Indians. They **migrated** to the area as early as 13,000 years ago. By the 1600s, the native people of Ohio were expert hunters and farmers.

That was around the time the first Europeans arrived in the area. They depended on the native people to show them how to obtain animal furs, which were very valuable. Europeans established trading posts to sell these furs. Over time, some of the posts became permanent settlements.

The presence of Europeans was a disaster for the American Indians. The settlers brought new diseases. Having never experienced these diseases, the native people got sick very easily, and many died. Tensions increased as more and more white settlers moved onto land that belonged to the native people. Many American

Tribes such as the Shawnee lived in what is now Ohio prior to the arrival of white settlers.

Indians were killed or forced to leave in wars such as the French and Indian War (1754–1763).

At the war's end, Ohio belonged to Great Britain. In 1775, the Revolutionary War broke out between the American colonists and the British. After the American victory in 1783, Ohio became part of the United States. It officially became a state in 1803. The name Ohio comes from an Iroquois word meaning "Great River."

In 1860, Ohio was the third-most populous state in the nation. When the US Civil War broke out in 1861, Ohio played a key role in the conflict. More than 100,000 Ohioans signed up for service in the first year of the war. In total, more than 300,000 took part in the war. Only two states sent more soldiers to battle.

One of the Ohioans who served was General Ulysses S. Grant. After the war, he went on to become the president of the United States. Four other Ohio veterans of the war also became president. In all, seven people born in Ohio have

Ulysses S. Grant was born in Point Pleasant, Ohio, and became the 18th US president.

held the office. For this reason, Ohio is known as "The Mother of Presidents."

Ohio also plays an important role in elections. From 1964 to 2016, every person elected US president won the state of Ohio. The state is sometimes referred to as "The Bellwether State."

A bellwether is something that can indicate a trend or result.

Ohio became an industrial state after the Civil War. In particular, it was known for manufacturing and technology. With the construction of the Saint Lawrence Seaway in 1958, Ohio could ship its products through the Great Lakes and to the rest of the world. These advances helped cities such as Cincinnati and Cleveland grow into the major population centers they are today.

Since the late 1900s, manufacturing has declined in Ohio. But it is still a big part of the economy, especially in the automotive industry. Ohio is also home to some of the country's largest health care and insurance companies.

From the banks of the Ohio River to the shores of Lake Erie, Ohio has many different people and places. But most of them have one thing in common: a love for the teams that represent them. Because of the state's central location, Ohio sports teams have many fierce **rivals**. When it comes to college football, the whole state gets together to cheer on the Buckeyes. But each of Ohio's major cities has pro teams that represent them, too.

OHIO'S PRO SPORTS TEAMS

MI

Lake Erie

IN

OHIO

Cleveland Indians
Cleveland Cavaliers
Cleveland Browns

N
W · E
S

PA

LEAGUE
■ MLB
■ MLS
■ NBA
■ NFL
■ NHL

Columbus Crew
Columbus Blue Jackets

Cincinnati Reds
Cincinnati Bengals

Ohio River

WV

KY

CHAPTER 2

TEAMS ACROSS OHIO

In a way, baseball as we know it began in Cincinnati. In 1869, the Cincinnati Red Stockings became the first all-professional team, meaning everyone on the team got paid. As a result, the team could attract the best players. That showed in the team's results. The Red Stockings won their first game of the 1869 season by a score of 45–9. They finished the year with a perfect 57–0 record.

The 1869 Red Stockings changed the future of baseball by paying players.

In 1880, the Red Stockings got kicked out of the National League (NL) for violating rules. But a new Red Stockings team was formed in 1882. That team is known today as the Cincinnati Reds. And today, all of the players in Major League Baseball (MLB) get paid.

The Reds have had some legendary teams and players. The club has won five World Series titles. Two of those came back-to-back, in 1975 and 1976. The powerful Reds teams of that era were known as "The Big Red Machine." Hall of Famers Johnny Bench, Joe Morgan, and Tony Pérez led the team, along with star hitter Pete Rose.

Up north, Cleveland had several different baseball teams in the 1800s. One of these was the Spiders, who posted the worst record in baseball history in 1899. The Spiders won only 20 games and lost 134. Their best pitcher went 4–30. But

A Cleveland pitcher Corey Kluber won his second American League Cy Young Award in 2017.

then a team from Grand Rapids, Michigan, moved to Cleveland in 1900. The next year, it became an original member of the American League (AL). Now known as the Indians, they've played in Cleveland ever since.

The Indians won the World Series in 1920 and 1948. They made it back in 1954 but lost. Then they didn't get back to the playoffs until 1995.

Led by slugger Jim Thome, the Indians made World Series appearances in 1995 and 1997. However, they couldn't break through to a title. The 2016 team also reached the World Series but suffered a heartbreaking Game 7 loss to the Chicago Cubs.

Ohio's baseball history goes back a long way. The same is true of its pro football history. The American Professional Football Association (APFA) was founded in 1920 at a car dealership in Canton, Ohio. Five of the original 11 APFA teams

► THINK ABOUT IT

In 2018, the Cleveland Indians announced they would get rid of their Chief Wahoo mascot because it was offensive to American Indians. Do you think all teams with native imagery should be forced to change? Why or why not?

Quarterback Otto Graham led the Cleveland Browns to seven championships, including three in the NFL.

were based in Ohio. The Akron Pros were the first league champion.

In 1922, the APFA renamed itself the National Football League (NFL). None of Ohio's original APFA teams are around today. Ohio's oldest NFL team is the Cleveland Browns. The Browns were founded in 1944 as a member of the All-America Football Conference. After that league folded, the Browns joined the NFL in 1950. Cleveland won the league championship in its first NFL season.

The Browns won three more championships through 1964. But their history after that was mostly disappointment. With a chance to go to the Super Bowl in 1987, the Browns collapsed. The Denver Broncos completed a 98-yard game-tying touchdown drive and then won in overtime. The Browns hit rock bottom in 2017 with a record of 0–16.

Cincinnati's NFL team has had a little more success. Former Browns owner Paul Brown founded the Bengals in 1967. They began play in 1968 as a team in the upstart American Football League (AFL). After two losing seasons, they joined the NFL when the leagues merged.

The Bengals played in the Super Bowl after the 1981 and 1988 seasons. However, they lost both times. The Bengals returned to the playoffs after a 15-year absence in 2005. Coach Marvin Lewis led

▲ Quicken Loans Arena in Cleveland is the place to be during a Cavaliers game.

the team to the playoffs seven times from 2005 to 2017. But the Bengals failed to win a single playoff game during that stretch.

For many years, the Cleveland Cavaliers were another Ohio team without much success. They played their first season in the National Basketball Association (NBA) in 1970. Although the Cavaliers had some good teams over the years, they always fell short of reaching the NBA Finals.

That changed when LeBron James arrived. The Cavaliers picked the Akron native first in the 2003 **draft**. The Cavs improved from 17 wins in the 2002–03 season to 35 wins in 2003–04. They reached their first NBA Finals in 2007 but lost.

When James left the Cavaliers to play for the Miami Heat in 2010, Cleveland quickly returned to its losing ways. But James returned in 2014–15. The next season, the Cavaliers broke through to win Cleveland's first major pro championship since the Browns won the NFL title in 1964.

Cleveland and Cincinnati were alone as Ohio's major league cities until 1996. That year, the Columbus Crew joined Major League Soccer (MLS) as one of the league's original teams. The Crew made history in 1999 as the first club in MLS to build a soccer-specific stadium. The Crew won their first MLS Cup in 2008.

Goalie Sergei Bobrovsky leads the Columbus Blue Jackets in many career statistics, including wins and saves.

The Columbus Blue Jackets joined the National Hockey League (NHL) in 2000. Their name pays tribute to the blue coats that Ohio soldiers wore during the Civil War. Rick Nash is the team leader in most categories, including games and points.

While some Ohio teams have struggled at times, they have been able to count on their loyal fans to stay with them through thick and thin.

BARRY LARKIN

Barry Larkin has been a Cincinnati legend ever since his days at Moeller High School. Larkin was born and raised in Cincinnati, and he played baseball, football, and basketball for the Moeller Crusaders. His hometown Reds drafted him out of high school. However, he decided to play for the University of Michigan baseball team instead. While there, he also played on the 1984 US Olympic baseball team that won a silver medal.

In 1985, after Larkin's third season at Michigan, the Reds drafted him again. After a short time in the minor leagues, he made his MLB debut on August 13, 1986. His first season as a starter was in 1988, when he hit .296 and stole 40 bases.

As a young player, Larkin made many fielding errors at shortstop. But by 1994, he was a Gold Glove Award winner and one of the best

A Only two players have played more games for the Reds than Barry Larkin.

shortstops in baseball. He won two more Gold Gloves the next two seasons.

Larkin hit .319 in 1995 and won the NL Most Valuable Player Award. In 1996, he became the first shortstop to hit 30 home runs and steal 30 bases. He also served as Reds team captain.

After playing all 19 of his MLB seasons with his hometown club, Larkin retired in 2004. He was elected to the National Baseball Hall of Fame in 2012.

CHAPTER 3

THE BUCKEYE STATE

O hio is a state that loves football, so it's no surprise that the state's **flagship** university has become one of the most successful programs in college football history. It has come a long way.

Ohio State University football dates back to 1890. On May 3 of that year, the Buckeyes football team played its first game. Ohio State went on the road to face Ohio Wesleyan University. The Buckeyes won in front of approximately 700 fans.

Quarterback Cardale Jones led the 2014 Ohio State Buckeyes to the national championship.

The Buckeyes hosted the College of Wooster for their first home game in Columbus. This time they lost 64–0.

Since those humble beginnings, the Buckeyes have won more than 700 games and dozens of Big Ten Conference titles. Under coach Urban Meyer, they won their eighth national championship in 2014. And attendance isn't measured in the hundreds anymore. It is measured in the hundreds of thousands. Ohio Stadium can fit more than 100,000 fans. That makes it one of the biggest college football stadiums. However, the University of Michigan's stadium is bigger.

The Wolverines and Buckeyes are huge rivals in everything, but especially football. The two have played every year since 1918. Known simply as "The Game," it is one of the greatest rivalries in college sports.

Few sporting events can draw a crowd as big as those at an Ohio State home football game.

There are seven other **Division I** football programs in Ohio. While not as popular statewide as the Buckeyes, these schools have loyal fans. Some regularly compete for bowl games. For instance, the University of Cincinnati Bearcats made the Orange Bowl after the 2008 season. One year later, they made the Sugar Bowl. The University of Toledo Rockets made 11 bowl game appearances from 2001 to 2017.

Football may be the most popular sport in Ohio, but it's far from the only sport. Ohio is home to 13 Division I men's basketball programs. Of these, Ohio State has been the most successful. It won the school's first national title in 1960. But in 1961 and 1962, Cincinnati won it all. And both times, the Bearcats beat the Buckeyes in the final. Ohio has several women's basketball teams as well. Ohio State was national runner-up in 1993.

In more recent years, Xavier University has been one of the best men's teams in the state. Since 2014, the Musketeers have regularly qualified for the national tournament. And in 2017, the Musketeers made a run to the Elite Eight. But as of 2018, they had never made it to a Final Four. Of all the schools in the country, Xavier has won the most tournament games without ever making it to the final round.

Xavier University, based in Cincinnati, missed the tournament only twice between 2001 and 2018.

Ohio is also home to three Division I men's college hockey teams. Hockey is one sport in which the Buckeyes do not rule Ohio. Through 2017, Bowling Green University was the only Ohio team to win a national title. Its championship occurred back in 1984. Both Bowling Green and Miami University also have more national tournament appearances than Ohio State.

CHAPTER 4

THE HOME OF AMERICAN FOOTBALL

Ohio helped change pro football forever in 1903. Before that time, most teams were made up of unpaid amateur players. The Massillon Tigers were one of these teams. Then in 1903, they lured away four professionals from Pittsburgh to play in a championship game against Akron. The Tigers won, and pro football in Ohio became more and more popular.

Huge crowds came out to watch Jim Thorpe lead the Canton Bulldogs in the early 1900s.

Massillon and Akron were two of several pro Ohio teams in the early 1900s. They played in a loose association of teams called the Ohio League. The Ohio League was one of the leagues that led to the creation of the NFL. Four teams from the league played in the first NFL season in 1920.

One of those Ohio League teams was the Canton Bulldogs. They won back-to-back NFL titles in 1922 and 1923. They also had legendary player Jim Thorpe. Plus, Canton was where the NFL was founded in 1920. That made Canton the perfect place to put the Pro Football Hall of Fame.

The Hall of Fame opened in 1963 and inducted its first 17 members that same year. Every summer, fans flock to Canton to see new Hall of Famers inducted at the Enshrinement Festival. The same weekend, the NFL season kicks off with

⬧ Each year, former NFL greats are enshrined at the Pro Football Hall of Fame in Canton, Ohio.

the first **preseason** game at nearby Tom Benson Hall of Fame Stadium.

The stadium is also home to another Ohio football tradition. High school football is incredibly popular in Ohio. The Canton stadium is the home of the Canton McKinley High School Bulldogs. Their football team dates back to 1894.

From then through 2017, the team had won more than 1,200 games and captured 12 state titles.

McKinley's chief rival is the Massillon Washington Tigers. They first played in 1894 in front of 200 fans. These days, they play for crowds of more than 20,000.

Glenville High School in Cleveland is a football factory. Between 2006 and 2017, Glenville had 13 players drafted into the NFL. That was the second most of any high school in the country.

Ohio's high schools send a huge number of players to college and pro football teams. From 2013 to 2017, Ohio high schools produced the

> # THINK ABOUT IT

How do you think high school football rivalries first developed?

fifth-most top **prospects recruited** by college football teams. In the history of the NFL, only Texas and California have produced more pro players than Ohio. And those states have much larger populations than the Buckeye State.

NFL PLAYERS' HOME STATES ◄

In 2017, Ohio was the birthplace of more active NFL players than any other state in the Midwest. Only four states produced more players who were active in the 2017 season.

No players	11 to 20 players	51 to 100 players
1 to 10 players	21 to 50 players	101 or more players

CHAPTER 5

BELIEVELAND AND BEYOND

One of Ohio's most well-known sports traditions is something its fans would rather not have. That's because, more often than not, Ohio pro teams are known for losing. In Cleveland, it even came to be called a curse.

The Cleveland Sports Curse began after the Browns won their last NFL title in 1964. In the curse's 52-year history, there wasn't much hope that it would end.

The Browns have mostly struggled to put together winning seasons since the 1960s.

The Indians had some great teams in the 1990s and reached the World Series twice. But they fell in six games in 1995 and seven games in 1997. The Browns were often bad on the field, and in 1995, the team moved to Baltimore and became the Ravens. A new Browns team joined the NFL in 1999. But the new Browns were one of the worst teams in the league. Even the Cavaliers gave fans very little to cheer about before LeBron James arrived in 2003. His departure to the Miami Heat in 2010 showed the curse was alive and well. But in 2014, James returned. Cleveland became known as "Believeland."

➤ THINK ABOUT IT

Would you still attend a game of your favorite team even if they weren't very good? Why or why not?

A huge crowd filled downtown Cleveland to celebrate the Cavaliers' 2016 NBA championship.

Fans believed in Cleveland sports but also in Cleveland itself. The city was once a manufacturing giant in the United States. Years of declining industry made Cleveland a shell of what it once was. The Cavs' 2016 playoff run gave Clevelanders a lot to be proud of. And when the team finally won that elusive title, the city celebrated. Approximately one million people came out for the Cavaliers' victory parade.

The Indians showed some belief of their own in 2016. They won their first AL championship since 1997 and went to the World Series. But they lost to a different "cursed" team, the Chicago Cubs. The Indians' title drought extended to 68 years, while the Cubs' ended at 108 years.

Fans take a lot of pride in being from Cleveland. It's why they root so passionately for Cleveland teams. In 2001, the Indians set a record for most consecutive sellouts. For 455 games in a row, the stands were full. The team even "retired" the number 455 to honor its passionate fans.

Fans have stuck with their teams during the bad times, too. The 2017 Browns didn't win a single game. Yet they still drew more fans than the Los Angeles Rams and Pittsburgh Steelers. Both of those teams had great seasons and made the playoffs.

The Browns also drew more fans than their downstate rivals, the Bengals. The Bengals and Browns share a common beginning. Paul Brown coached them both. But the teams have had very different histories. The Bengals played in two Super Bowls during a time the Browns never made one.

OHIO'S BIGGEST STADIUMS

Fans show up to cheer on Ohio sports teams at some big stadiums.

1. Ohio Stadium (Ohio State football): 104,944
2. FirstEnergy Stadium (Browns): 67,895
3. Paul Brown Stadium (Bengals): 65,515
4. Great American Ballpark (Reds): 42,271
5. Nippert Stadium (Cincinnati football): 40,000
6. Progressive Field (Indians): 35,225

Connected by Interstate 71, Cincinnati and Cleveland are natural rivals. Cincinnati is a southern river town, while Cleveland is a manufacturing town on the Great Lakes. Culturally, they could be in different states.

Columbus is between them. It is another working-class city like Cleveland. Those roots are why its MLS team got the nickname "Crew." The original club badge even depicted workers wearing hard hats. Columbus is thought of as the "third city" in Ohio. But Crew fans embrace this identity. They like to say Columbus and the Crew are "massive." Even if Columbus isn't as big as Cincinnati and Cleveland, the fans know it's still a big, important city.

This is particularly true in soccer. The Crew's home stadium has often played host to the US men's national team. Columbus has provided

△ Columbus Crew fans are known for their passionate support of their team and their city.

a great home-field advantage for the US team, especially when the weather is cold. A 2001 match with Mexico was called "The Cold War" for its freezing-cold conditions.

Ohio teams might not win as often as teams from Boston or New York. But their fans are every bit as passionate. If a team is taking the field in Ohio, fans will be there to support them.

LEBRON JAMES

When LeBron James was in high school, the people of Akron knew he was going to be special. It wasn't long before the whole world knew it, too.

James was featured on the cover of *Sports Illustrated* magazine when he was a junior at St. Vincent–St. Mary High School. The next year, the Cleveland Cavaliers chose him first overall in the 2003 NBA Draft.

James was named **Rookie** of the Year and became the youngest player to score 40 points in an NBA game. He made his first All-Star Game in 2005 and had not missed another one through 2018. "King James" made the Cavaliers winners again and became a local hero.

But in 2010, James decided to leave Cleveland and join the Miami Heat. His decision was broadcast on national TV. Cavaliers fans turned on James as the Cavaliers became one of the

🔺 LeBron James combines the size of a forward with the skills of a point guard.

NBA's worst teams. Meanwhile, James won two titles in Miami.

In 2014, James announced he was coming back to the Cavaliers. And in his first season back, he led the team to the NBA Finals. Then in 2016, he led them to a championship. The hometown kid had finally won a title for Cleveland. With the King back in town, the Cavaliers remained one of the best teams in the NBA.

FOCUS ON
OHIO

Write your answers on a separate piece of paper.

1. Write a paragraph that summarizes why Cleveland became known as Believeland.

2. Which Ohio team is your favorite? Why?

3. Which men's basketball team has won the most tournament games without reaching the Final Four?
   - **A.** Xavier
   - **B.** Ohio State
   - **C.** Cincinnati

4. Why did the Pro Football Hall of Fame end up in Canton?
   - **A.** Canton offered the most money.
   - **B.** Canton had a long pro football history.
   - **C.** No other cities were big enough.

Answer key on page 48.

GLOSSARY

Division I
The top level of college sports in the United States.

draft
A system that allows teams to acquire new players coming into a league.

economy
A system of goods, services, money, and jobs.

flagship
The largest or most important part of an organization.

migrated
Moved from one region to another.

preseason
The time before the regular season. Preseason games do not count in the standings.

prospects
Players who are likely to be successful in the future.

recruited
Persuaded someone to attend a college, usually to play sports.

rivals
Teams or players that have an intense and ongoing competition against one another.

rookie
A professional athlete in his or her first year.

TO LEARN MORE

BOOKS

Hamilton, John. *Ohio: The Buckeye State*. Minneapolis: Abdo Publishing, 2017.

Morey, Allan. *The Cincinnati Bengals Story*. Minneapolis: Bellwether Media, 2017.

Whiting, Jim. *Cleveland Cavaliers*. Mankato, MN: Creative Education, 2017.

NOTE TO EDUCATORS

Visit **www.focusreaders.com** to find lesson plans, activities, links, and other resources related to this title.

INDEX

Answer Key: 1. Answers will vary; **2.** Answers will vary; **3.** A; **4.** B